# My World of Science

# MAGNETS

## Angela Royston

Heinemann Library
Chicago, Illinois

© 2001 Reed Educational & Professional Publishing
Published by Heinemann Library,
an imprint of Reed Educational & Professional Publishing,
Chicago, Illinois

Customer Service  888-454-2279

Visit our website at www.heinemannlibrary.com

Designed by bigtop
Originated by Ambassador Litho
Printed and bound in Hong Kong/China

06 05 04
10 9 8 7 6 5 4

**Library of Congress Cataloging-in-Publication Data**
Royston, Angela.
  Magnets.
    p. cm. -- (My world of science)
Includes bibliographical references and index
  ISBN 1-58810-243-2 (lib. bdg.)          ISBN 1-4034-0042-3 (pbk. bdg.)
  1. Magnets--Juvenile literature. 2. Magnetism--Juvenile literature.
[1. Magnets. 2. Magnetism.] I. Title.
  QC757.5 .R695 2001
  538'.4--dc21
                              00-012872

Acknowledgments
The author and publishers are grateful to the following for permission to reproduce copyright material:

M. Barlow/Trip, p. 9; Trevor Clifford, pp. 4, 5, 6, 7, 8, 10, 11, 12, 13, 16, 17, 19, 20, 21, 22, 23, 24, 25, 26, 27, 28, 29; Photodisc, p. 14; Powerstock Photo Library, p. 15; Stockshot, p. 18.

Cover photograph reproduced with permission of Robert Harding.

Every effort has been made to contact copyright holders of any material reproduced in this book.
Any omissions will be rectified in subsequent printings if notice is given to the publisher.

Some words are shown in bold, **like this.** You can find out what they mean by looking in the glossary.

# Contents

# What Is a Magnet?

A magnet can pull some things toward it. The magnet has a **force** in it that you cannot see. You can only see what the force does.

This fishing rod has a magnet tied to the end of the line. The magnet on the line pulls the magnet on the fish toward it. That is why the fish stick to the line.

# What Is Magnetic?

Magnets only work on some kinds of **materials.** If something is pulled toward a magnet, it is said to be **magnetic.** A paper clip is magnetic.

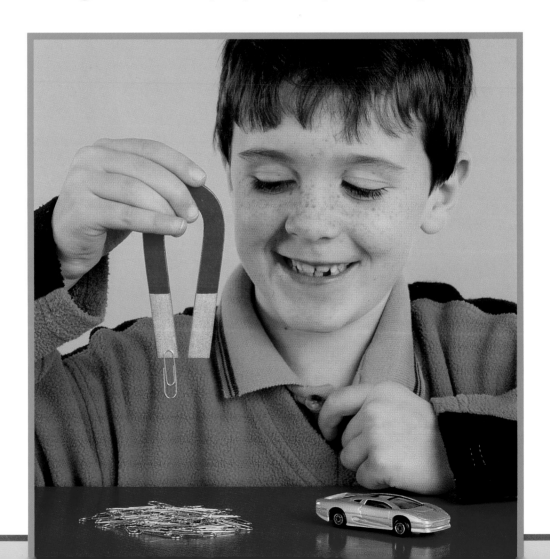

This girl is using a magnet to test whether things are magnetic or not. The leaf is not magnetic because the magnet cannot lift it.

# Magnetic Metals

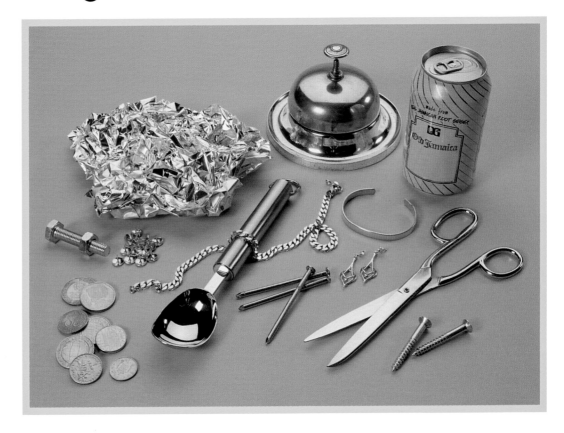

Most metals are hard, strong, and shiny. There are many different kinds of metal. All the things in the picture are made of metal. Only some metals are **magnetic.**

Iron and steel are metals that are magnetic. Iron and steel are used to make many things, including trains, bridges, nails, and paper clips.

# Shapes of Magnets

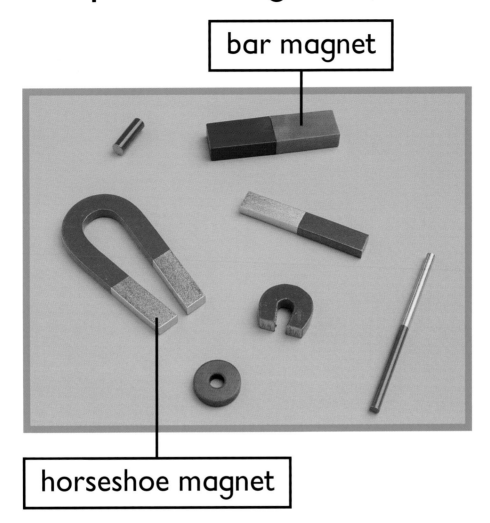

bar magnet

horseshoe magnet

Magnets can be any shape. The most common shapes for magnets are horseshoes and bars.

The magnets that stick to a refrigerator have all kinds of shapes. The magnets stick to the door of the refrigerator because it is made of steel.

# Testing Strength

This girl is testing which magnet is stronger. She puts a nail on a line on a piece of paper. Then she moves the first magnet slowly toward the nail.

When the nail moves to the magnet, she marks where the magnet is. The strongest magnet pulls the nail from farther away.

# Using Magnets

A **recycling center** uses magnets to separate aluminum cans from steel cans. Only the steel cans are **attracted** to the magnets.

Magnets are used to move heavy pieces of metal. This crane has a huge magnet on the end. It can lift and move metal that is too heavy for people to move.

# Magnets at Home

The knives in the picture are sticking to a **magnetic** knife holder. That means the knives are made of iron or steel.

The door of a refrigerator has a rubber strip that covers a magnet. The magnet under the rubber pulls the door closed. The rubber strip **seals** the door to keep the cold air in the refrigerator.

rubber magnet cover

# Compasses

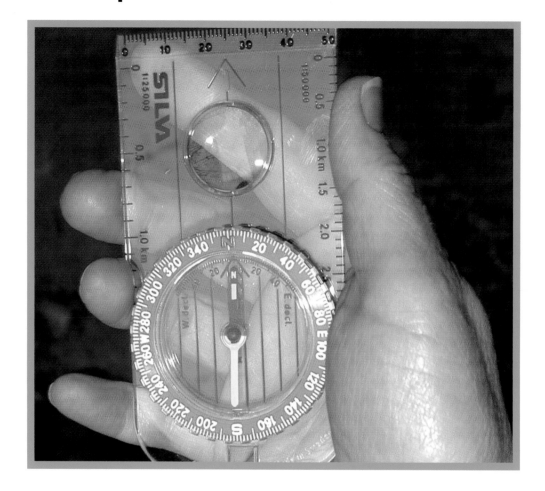

A **compass** uses a magnet to tell you which direction you are moving. The compass needle always points north. Hikers and sailors use compasses.

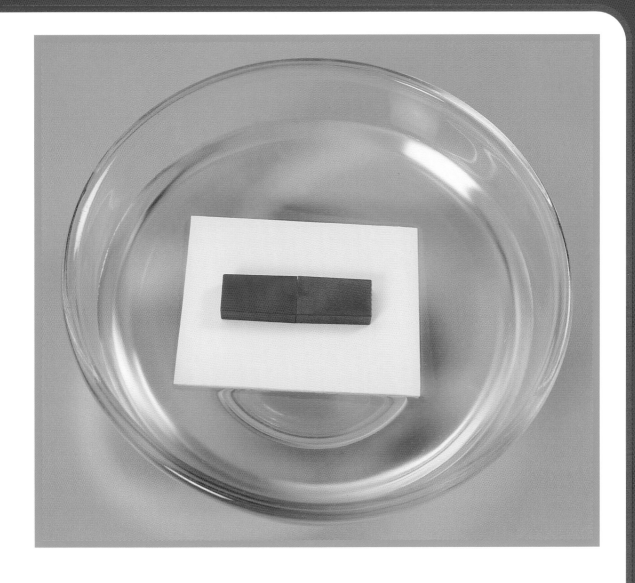

This is a homemade compass. It floats and can turn on the water. One end of the magnet points north and the other end points south.

# Magnetic Poles

This magnet was placed on top of a pile of pins. The strongest parts of the magnet **attract** the most pins. What is stronger—the end or the middle?

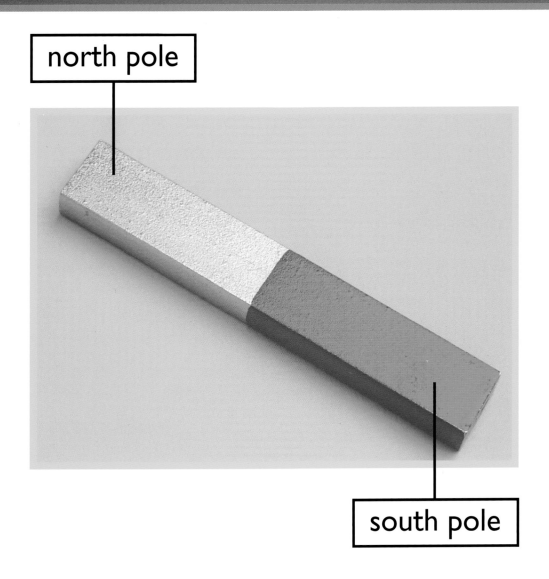

north pole

south pole

The ends of a magnet are called the poles. One end is called the north pole and the other end is called the south pole.

# Poles that Attract

The two poles of a magnet are not the same. The north pole of one magnet **attracts** the south pole of another magnet. You can feel them pulling toward each other.

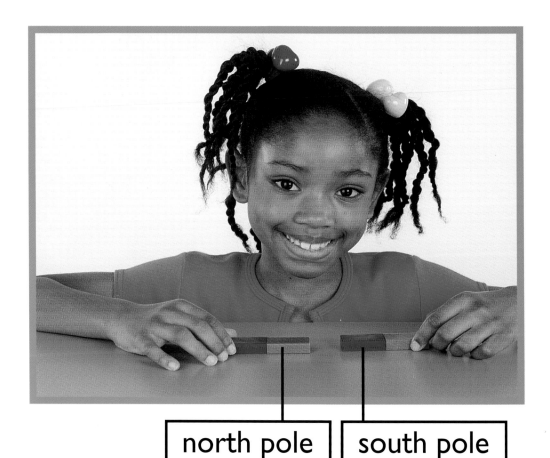

| north pole | south pole |

The attraction is very strong.
Sometimes it can be hard to
pull the magnets apart!

# Poles that Push Away

Sometimes magnets push each other away. You cannot make a north pole stick to another north pole. Two south poles also **repel** each other.

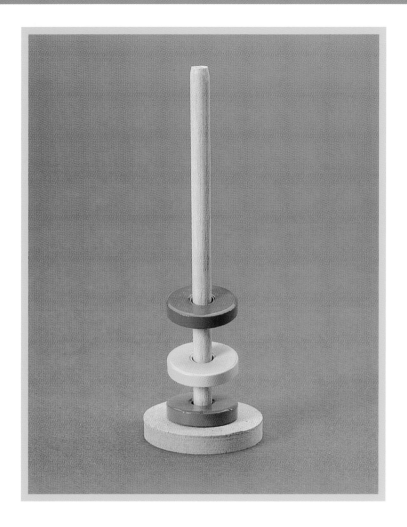

These magnets are floating above each other. The poles are at the tops and bottoms of the ring magnets. They are pushing each other away.

# Magnetized Metals

When iron or steel sticks to a magnet, it becomes magnetized. This means it becomes a magnet too. The first paper clip magnetizes the second paper clip.

The stronger the magnet, the longer the chain of paper clips. If you remove the magnet, the chain falls apart. The paper clips are no longer magnetized.

# Making a Magnet

You can make a magnet that lasts.
This boy is rubbing a nail with a
magnet. He rubs it about 50 times,
in the same direction.

The nail becomes a magnet. It is strong enough to pick up this paper clip. It can magnetize the paper clip too.

# Glossary

**attract**  pull toward something

**compass** tool that uses a magnet to tell you which direction you are moving

**force**  power that makes things move

**magnetic**  something that can be pulled toward a magnet

**material**  what something is made of

**recycling center**  place where something old is made into something new

**repel**  push away from something

**seal**  to close something so tightly that nothing can get in or out of it

# More Books to Read

Branley, Franklyn M. *What Makes a Magnet?* New York: HarperCollins Children's Book Group, 1996.

Fowler, Allan. *What Magnets Can Do.* Danbury, Conn.: Children's Press, 1995.

Madgwick, Wendy. *Magnets and Sparks.* Austin, Tex.: Raintree Steck-Vaughn, 1999.

# Index